DATE		

DISCARD

baby GIFTS

SIMPLE HEIRLOOMS TO MAKE AND GIVE

baby GIFTS

by Ethel Brennan

Photographs by Laurie Frankel

CHRONICLE BOOKS

SAN FRANCISCO

Text copyright © 2002 by Ethel Brennan.
Photographs copyright © 2002 by Laurie Frankel.
Illustrations copyright © 2002 by Nicole Kaufman.
All rights reserved. No part of this book may be
reproduced in any form without written permission
from the publisher.

Library of Congress Cataloging-in-Publication Data
available.

ISBN: 0-8118-3229-5

Manufactured in China

Designed by Laurie Frankel
Styling by Ethel Brennan

Distributed in Canada by Raincoast Books
9050 Shaughnessy Street
Vancouver, British Columbia V6P 6E5

10 9 8 7 6 5 4 3 2 1

Chronicle Books LLC
85 Second Street
San Francisco, California 94105

www.chroniclebooks.com

contents

introduction

The months preceding the birth of a baby are filled with excitement and anticipation. Parents-to-be spend these precious days decorating the nursery, preparing the home for the new addition, and dreaming about the future. Friends and family take time to make gifts that will become cherished heirlooms—a knit cap and booties, a baby quilt, that special toy. There is something magical in these tokens of a child's beginnings. By making and giving these baby gifts we celebrate a new life. In the careful creation and collection of these treasures we become keepers of both the future and the history of our families.

My little brother was born when I was four. I still remember many of the baby gifts that friends and family gave to my parents—a small butterfly quilt, a handheld bassinet lined with vintage French linens and trimmed with hand-crocheted lace. I remember my mother knitting him an entire wardrobe of soft wool booties, caps, and sweaters, which I promptly tried on my dolls. Now, nearly thirty years later, our family still has many of those treasures, packed away in readiness for the next generation of babies.

Baby Gifts offers inspiration and simple, step-by-step instructions for a wide variety of projects, from adorable clothes to clever storage solutions. Some of the creations in this book may become heirlooms, to be passed down from one generation to the next, while the purely practical gifts will be welcome necessities for the new parents. Whether you are a seasoned crafter or you have never made anything in your life, you'll find a gift in these pages that you will enjoy making and giving.

Begin with "Getting Started," a section that outlines the various tools and materials needed to complete the projects and offers clear instructions for basic techniques. "Chapter 1: Wardrobe Classics" offers such delightful apparel as customized One-of-a-Kind Onesies, leak-resistant Baby Bloomers, and a colorful Snuggle Suit. "Chapter 2: Nursery Trimmings" turns to baby's room, suggesting practical additions such as the Happy Hamper and the Tidy-up Nursery Organizer as well as furnishings like a brightly Painted Dresser and Polka-dot Chair. New parents need a lot of utilitarian accessories, and "Chapter 3: Pretty Practicalities" focuses on fun versions of standards like No-sew Bibs, a Baby Bath Kit, and handy Embroidered Nursing Cloths. Finally, "Chapter 4: Toys and Things" offers up colorful and safe playthings for the little one, from Squeezable Blocks to a Snuggle Bear Blanket.

Making a baby gift can be as simple as embellishing a purchased item of clothing or as adventurous as sanding, painting, and decorating nursery furniture. **Baby Gifts** offers something for everyone, from the practical to the purely nostalgic, the silly to the serious. My hope is that you will enjoy creating the projects from these pages—so much of the joy in receiving a gift comes from the love put into making it.

getting
STARTED

getting started

The key to successful crafting is preparation. Before starting a project, make a list of all the things you will need. This will help you streamline your shopping and gather all your tools and materials in one trip. Hardware, fabric, and art supply stores will have everything you need for the most basic gifts; vintage shops, flea markets, and antique malls provide unusual treasures and boundless inspiration for more ambitious undertakings. For the inexpensive baby clothes and daily necessities to which you'll be adding a personal touch, shop large discount stores, clothing outlets, and department stores at sale time.

While all the craft items in this book are presented with specific instructions, I hope readers will be inspired to create their own versions, using the book as a guide for techniques. One needn't be an experienced crafter to make the projects in these pages. Still, if you are a beginner, particularly to the world of sewing, I recommend that you familiarize yourself with the materials and perhaps even take a few practice runs with the needle and thread. Following are the essential supplies you will need, as well as some basic techniques that are helpful to know.

SEWING AND CRAFT ESSENTIALS

The craft instructions assume you have on hand these basic items:

fabric scissors

needles and assorted thread for hand sewing

ruler

safety pins

scissors for paper and plastic

sewing machine

steam iron and ironing board

straight pins

tape measure

SPECIAL MATERIALS FROM CRAFT, FABRIC, AND ART SUPPLY STORES

These items may be needed for individual craft projects:

bias tape

colored tissue paper

cotton swabs

decoupage medium, such as Mod-Podge

disappearing-ink marking pen

drop cloth

embroidery needles

embroidery templates

embroidery thread in assorted colors

eyelet kit

fabric paints

fishing line or clear filament thread, medium gauge, available in craft stores

hammer

headliner foam, available in the upholstery department of craft and fabric stores

hot-glue gun and glue

hot-iron transfer templates

iron-on double-sided fusible tape

iron-on pencil

iron-on vinyl

masking tape

paintbrushes of assorted sizes and types

pinking shears, zigzag or scalloped edge

polyester or cotton batting and filling

polyurethane sealant

repositionable spray glue

rubber gloves

rubber stamps and ink pads in various colors

sandpaper

seam ripper or small nail scissors

self-adhesive linen or fabric tape

small embroidery ring

stencils of letters or other shapes

utility knife and extra blades

SEWING AND EMBROIDERING TECHNIQUES

With a few simple stitches and some basic techniques, you're on your way to sewing and embroidering like the pros.

Hand sewing

To knot the thread in your needle before beginning to sew, match up the thread ends and make a loop by bringing the ends up and crossing them over the threads, about ½ inch from the ends. Slip the ends through the loop and pull taut. To use a single strand, knot only one end of the thread.

The most utilitarian hand stitch is the straight stitch (see page 17). Use this stitch in place of most machine stitching.

To finish a hand-stitched seam, make a small final stitch without pulling it taut, leaving a loop. Bring the needle back through to the loop side of the fabric, pass it through the loop a couple of times, and pull taut, creating a knot.

Machine sewing

When sewing a seam, edge, or decoration by machine, whether you are using a straight or a zigzag stitch, always backstitch ¼ inch at the beginning and again at the end of a line of stitching to secure. The only exception is the running stitch (see page 16). It is used as a basting stitch, which you will want to remove in the end, or as a gathering stitch, which calls for unsecured ends.

Be sure to choose the right sewing machine needle for the fabric you are using. Follow the manufacturer's indications on a pack of assorted needles.

Basting stitch

Basting is the single most important step when sewing. This temporary stitching, used to hold fabric pieces in place for the final sewing, is essential when working with slippery or unwieldy fabrics such as silk, nylon, or fleece. Skipping this step leads to unaligned seams and mismatched corners. To hand baste, first pin the fabric pieces together. Hand sew the seam with long, straight stitches, about ½ inch apart, working about ¾ inch in from the cut edges; knot the end of thread when finished and remove pins. To machine baste, use a running stitch (see page 16). Always remove basting stitches from finished projects.

Blanket stitch

This hand-sewn stitch secures interior seams or decorative exterior seams using yarn or embroidery thread. Thread a needle and knot one end of the thread or yarn. Sewing close to the cut edge of the seam, bring the needle through both pieces of the fabric. Make a ¼ inch straight stitch along the seam but don't

pull it tight, instead leaving a small loop. Slip the needle back through the loop and pull taut. Make another ¼ inch straight stitch and repeat the process, keeping the stitching aligned along the top of the seam.

Chain stitch

This embroidery stitch is ideal for outlines and letters. Cut a length of embroidery thread, separate a single or double strand, and knot the ends together. Working along the template line, bring the needle up through the wrong side of the fabric. Re-insert the needle right next to where it came through. Pull the thread through, stopping when you have a small loop on the right side of the fabric. Bring the needle back up through the fabric about ¼ inch forward, pass it through the loop, and pull taut. Re-insert the needle, again right next to where it emerged, creating a second loop within the first. Continue this process, creating a series of small, interlinked loop stitches.

Clipping seams

Clipping leaves curved seams smooth and flat and brings corners to crisp, perfect points. For a curved seam, carefully make several cuts in the seam allowance perpendicular to the line of stitching but stopping just short of it. Be careful not to cut the stitches. For a corner, cut a small V into the seam, just to the stitches, removing a small triangle of fabric.

French knot stitch

This embroidery stitch is perfect for creating a textured look to fill in surface areas. Use two strands of embroidery thread knotted together at the ends. Bring the needle up through the wrong side of the fabric and hold the thread down with your thumb. At the stitch, wrap the thread around the needle twice. Immediately re-insert the needle right next to the stitch, holding the thread taut, and pull the needle through to the wrong side. Make the second knot right next to the first. Continue this process until the surface of the template is filled in.

1

2

3

Hem stitch

This invisible, hand-sewn stitch is used to sew hems down. First fold the raw edge down ¼ inch and iron down, then fold the hem to the correct length and iron in position. Begin sewing at a seam and bring the needle through the hem, very close to the edge. Make a ⅜ inch stitch and pluck the needle through the back side of the fabric, making a tiny stitch. Avoid going through to the right side of the fabric. Repeat these stitches all around the hem.

Pin-prick stitch

This hand-sewn stitch is useful for tacking down fabric or sewing on trim and ribbons. Bring the needle and thread up through to the right side of the fabric and make a tiny "pin-prick" stitch, catching just a thread or two of the fabric weave, and go back through to the wrong side of the fabric. Make stitches ¼ inch apart.

Running stitch

This machine stitch is used for basting and gathering. Set the machine to the longest straight-stitch setting and sew along the edge of the fabric. If gathering the fabric, gently pull on one of the thread ends and the fabric will gather.

Satin stitch

This embroidery stitch creates a smooth, flat look, ideal for filling in surfaces. Using two strands of embroidery thread knotted at the ends, make a series of side-by-side stitches so close together that they form a continuous field of color. Following a template, bring the needle up through to the front

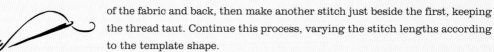

of the fabric and back, then make another stitch just beside the first, keeping the thread taut. Continue this process, varying the stitch lengths according to the template shape.

Slip stitch

A hidden stitch, this one is good for detailed hand sewing, such as sewing in linings or closing the opening through which a piece was turned inside out. The trick is to sew the seam from the inside. Use pin-prick stitches through both pieces of fabric, the longer stitch running in between the two pieces.

Straight stitch

The straight stitch is the most commonly used stitch in sewing. Sewing machines provide several lengths to choose from; I usually work with a medium length. To hand sew a straight stitch, thread the needle and knot the ends together. Bring the needle up from one side of the two fabric pieces and make a ⅛ inch stitch. Repeat. Short, close-together stitches are the most secure.

Using embroidery templates

For the best embroidery results, use a transfer template as a guide for your stitches. There are several methods for transferring images onto fabric, and the materials needed are readily available in craft and fabric stores. The simplest way to transfer templates onto fabric is to use ready-made iron-on transfers specifically for embroidery and needlepoint. The transfers range from simple to complex and include traditional designs like monograms. If you're not afraid of drawing, sketch your own template, using an iron-on transfer pencil, onto lightweight plain paper. Remember to draw the design in mirror image, especially if letters are involved. To transfer the templates in the back of the book, trace them with the transfer pencil onto paper. Position the traced template, transfer-side down, on the fabric and use a dry, medium-heat iron to transfer the design. Finally, for a quick design or to trace a simple stuffed-animal face, use a disappearing-ink marking pen with a fine or regular point. The image will actually vanish after several hours or can be removed with a little water.

CHAPTER ONE

wardrobe

CLASSICS

baby bloomers

Pretty, inexpensive cotton fabrics can easily be waterproofed with iron-on vinyl, available in craft and fabric stores. These colorful, water-resistant bloomers provide active babies with a little extra protection from leaks. Make a stack of them, one for every day of the week. For a professionally finished look, use a wide zigzag stitch when sewing the elastic onto the waist and legs.

template (page 102)

⅓ yard clear iron-on vinyl, in matte or gloss

25-by-18-inch rectangle lightweight cotton fabric

40 inches of ½-inch-wide lingerie elastic, cut into one 18-inch piece and two 10-inch pieces

Photocopy the template onto plain white paper, enlarging 250 percent. Cut out and set aside.

Following the manufacturer's directions, apply the iron-on vinyl to the wrong side of the fabric. When the vinyl has cooled, pin the template to the fabric and carefully cut out. Remove pins.

Lay the cut-out pants flat, right side of fabric facing up, and fold in half, matching up the waistband sides. The wrong side of the fabric will be facing out. Pin along each of the two sides and sew, leaving a ⅜ inch seam allowance. Remove pins and trim the seam allowance to ¼ inch. The large opening at the top is the waist. The two smaller openings at the bottom are the leg holes.

To make the waistband, match one end of the 18-inch piece of elastic to a side seam. The decorative edge of the elastic should peek over the edge of the waist. Begin machine sewing the elastic to the fabric by backstitching ¼ inch, then proceed forward, using a long stitch length. After the first inch, firmly feed the fabric through the machine while simultaneously pulling the unsewn elastic taut. This creates a gathered effect. Continue this process around the circumference of the waist. When you are finished the elastic ends should overlap by no more than an inch. Stitch back and forth over the ends several times to secure the stitching. Repeat the process with a 10-inch piece of elastic for each of the two leg holes.

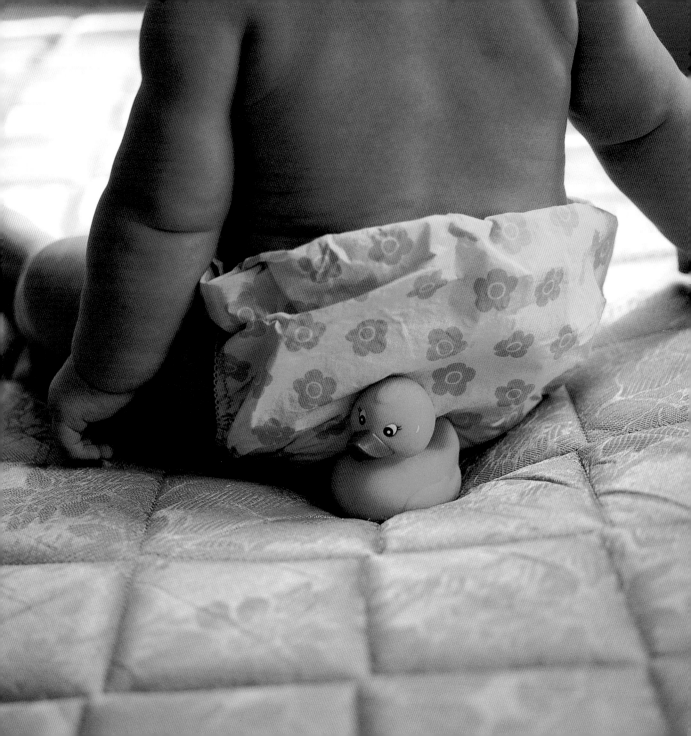

snow hat and socks

Make these cozy accessories from a lightweight knit in a soft pastel color, and wrap them up in sparkly tissue paper. The following measurements are for a newborn, but it's simple to make the pieces larger to accommodate an older infant. These are easily sewn by hand or machine.

To make the hat, fold the 14-inch-by-12½-inch rectangle in half lengthwise with the wrong side of fabric facing outward. Baste the long edge together and machine sew, leaving a ⅜-inch seam allowance. Remove basting thread.

Turn the tube right-side out and work one end up through the inside of the tube until the raw edges meet. This end is the top of the hat. Flatten the tube with the seam in the center, rather than at an edge. Starting about 2 inches down on each side, cut upwards in an arc to round off the raw edge corners of the hat (see illustration).

From the center top of the hat, sew a ¼-inch tapered seam 2 inches down on both the front and the back sides, dividing the hat top into quarters (see illustration). Baste the top closed and sew, leaving a ⅜-inch seam allowance. Remove basting thread. Trim the top with the pinking shears, turn the hat right-side out, and fold up the bottom edge.

To make the socks, follow the instructions for the hat, but skip the steps for the tapered seams. To hand sew both hat and booties, follow the instructions using a small blanket stitch (see page 14), but do not trim the seams.

½ yard lightweight knit fabric, such as jersey, cut into one 14-by-12½-inch rectangle and two 12-by-4-inch rectangles, long edges running with the fabric grain

pinking shears

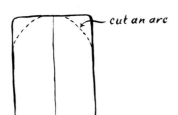

cut an arc

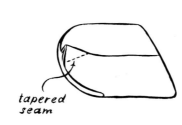

tapered seam

cashmere sweater

Here is a simple, no-knit sweater made from cashmere and trimmed with soft velvet ribbon. Flea markets, thrift and vintage shops, discount designer clothing outlets, and high-end fabric stores are excellent sources of cashmere. Buy it new or donate a soft adult-size sweater to the cause. If you don't have a sewing machine, you can assemble and stitch the entire sweater by hand, using a blanket stitch for the edges. The sweater measurements here are for a newborn; enlarge as needed to suit an older infant or even a toddler.

½ yard cashmere cut into one 9-by-8-inch rectangle (back), two 4½-by-8-inch rectangles (front sections), and two 7-by-4-inch rectangles (sleeves)

about 1½ yards ¼-inch-wide velvet ribbon, cut into one 18-inch, one 10-inch, and two 8½-inch pieces

½ yard ½-inch-wide silk ribbon, cut in half

To assemble the sweater, lay the 9-by-8-inch rectangle flat, with the 9-inch sides at the top and bottom and the right side of the knit facing up. Match up the two front panels to the back at the 8-inch sides, right sides of knit facing (see illustration, page 26).

Baste the front panels to the back panels along the shoulders, leaving 4 inches (2 inches per panel) for the neck opening. Sew, leaving a ¼-inch seam allowance. Remove basting thread. Turn right-side out.

For the sleeves, fold a 7-by-4-inch rectangle in half lengthwise to find the center point of the short edge. Pin the center point of the sleeve to the sweater body at the shoulder seam, right sides of fabric facing (see illustration, page 26). Baste the sleeve to the body, remove pin, then sew, leaving a ¼-inch seam allowance. Turn sweater inside out. Baste the long side of the sleeve closed and continue basting down the side of the sweater, attaching the panels together. Sew, leaving a ⅜-inch seam allowance. Remove basting

continued

thread. Fold over the cuff edge of the sleeve ¼ inch. Fold again, and sew down with a hem stitch. Repeat to attach the second sleeve. Turn the sweater right-side out and gently press with a cool iron.

If your machine has a zigzag stitch, use it to sew the sleeve and side seams again, close to the raw edge, being careful not to overlap the straight stitches. Sew a zigzag stitch around the neck, front edges, and bottom edge of the sweater. If your machine does not have a zigzag stitch, secure the seams and edges using a blanket stitch (see page 14).

To add the ribbon trim, turn the sweater right-side out and pin the 8½-inch lengths of velvet ribbon along each front edge. Secure using a pin-prick stitch (see page 16) and remove pins. Repeat for the bottom edge trim using the 18-inch length of ribbon, but this time fold the ends of the ribbon over, finishing the front bottom corners.

To finish the neck with its ribbon ties, use the same method as above to attach the 10-inch length of velvet ribbon along the neckline edge, and fold the ends over the corners. Pin a piece of silk ribbon to each end of the neckline. Fold the neckline over so that the velvet ribbon is completely inside the neckline and pin in place. Slip-stitch the neckline corners closed, securing the silk ribbon ties. Finally, slip-stitch the velvet ribbon to the inside of the sweater neckline all the way around.

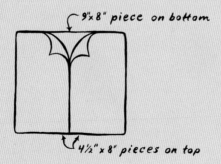

9"x 8" piece on bottom

4½" x 8" pieces on top

felt cap and booties

The perfect gift for a stylish baby, these irresistible booties and matching cap are trimmed with decorative seams. Use pinking shears with zigzag edges or the more unusual scalloped-edge shears to finish the seams. These booties can also be made with velcro or ribbon, if desired. Please make sure buttons are securely attached so that curious little ones cannot pull them off.

Photocopy the templates onto plain white paper, enlarging 150 percent. Cut out.

To make the booties, pin the templates to the felt and cut out the top of the bootie and the sole. The inner cutout of the bootie top will form the ankle straps, so be sure to follow the cutting lines on the template precisely. Remove pins. Repeat to cut out top and sole for the second bootie.

Fold one top piece in half lengthwise and secure with a pin. Sew the back edges together, leaving a ⅜-inch seam allowance, and remove pin. Trim the seam allowance with the pinking shears. Press the seam open and stitch each side down, ⅛ inch from the central seam.

Fit the edges of the sole to the bottom edge of the bootie top. Pin and sew, leaving a ⅜-inch seam allowance all the way around, removing pins as you go. Trim the seam allowances with the pinking shears. Make the second bootie in the same way.

Hold a hot iron just above, but not touching, the booties. Steam the booties, set the iron aside, and gently tug at the straps to loosen and lengthen them

continued

templates (page 101)

¼ yard wool blend felt, or 4 precut 9-by-12-inch felt pieces

pinking shears, zigzag or scalloped edge

2 small buttons, about ¼ inch in diameter

¼ yard lightweight fabric such as china silk, for lining

small bow, pom-pom, or other decoration

slightly. Decide on left and right booties, and sew buttons to the tips of the two outside straps. Cut small slits in the tips of the opposite straps, just large enough for the button to slip through. If desired, finish each buttonhole by hand-stitching the edges.

To add a little extra shape to each bootie, hold a hot iron an inch away from the booties and steam. Set the iron aside and, working quickly from the inside with your fingertips, gently sculpt and round the toe. Repeat as necessary.

To make the hat, pin the template to the felt and cut. Repeat until you have four pieces. Pin the panels together one by one, pointed tips matching up. Baste the panels together, remove pins, and sew, leaving a ⅜-inch seam allowance. Remove basting thread. Trim the seam allowances with the pinking shears and set aside. Leave the hat inside out.

To make the lining, cut four template pieces from the silk. Assemble the lining the same way as the hat, but making sure the right sides of the fabric are facing. Press the seams open and turn right-side out.

Turn the hat inside out and fit the lining inside, right-sides facing, seams matching. The wrong side of the lining should show when you look in. Pin the lining and the hat together around the brim and baste, leaving a 3-inch segment unsewn. Remove pins.

Sew around the basted edge, leaving a ⅜-inch seam allowance. Remove basting thread. Turn the hat and lining right-side out through the 3-inch opening. The lining will fit nicely inside the hat.

Press the opening of the hat flat and slip-stitch the remainder of the seam closed (see page 17). Attach the top of the lining to the top of the hat with a pin-prick stitch (see page 16). Working from the inside, secure the decoration to the top of the hat using a pin-prick stitch.

fancy pants

Search fabric stores, flea markets, and vintage shops for cute, unusual treasures to dress up everyday clothes. Replacing plain buttons with fanciful ones or sewing trim, ribbon, and appliqués around cuffs is a simple and fun way to personalize a tiny pair of jeans. It is absolutely essential to sew items on securely, so they do not become dangerous chew toys for a curious baby.

overalls (or any article of clothing)

ribbon

trim such as fringe, lace, or pom-poms

flower, butterfly, or other sew-on or iron-on appliqués

Measure the circumference of the leg cuffs and cut lengths of ribbon or trim to fit. Pin in place and sew, using a slip stitch or pin-prick stitch. Remove pins. Repeat with more ribbon at other places on the garment as desired.

Sew or iron on a scattering of delicate butterflies or flowers near the bands of ribbon or trim. Any number of combinations can look delightful. I like to use bands of rickrack with little bees or other animal appliqués above the trim.

one-of-a-kind onesies

A baby can never have too many cotton onesies and plain T-shirts. Buy a pack of them and personalize them with embroidery, decorative trim, and paint prints. When using appliqués or other decorations make sure to attach them securely so that baby cannot pull them off.

1 multiple pack plain white onesies or T-shirts, side-snap or pullover

FOR EMBROIDERY:

embroidery templates

cotton embroidery thread

embroidery needle

FOR DECORATIVE TRIMMING:

small silk ribbon butterflies or other appliqués

trim or ribbon

FOR PAINT PRINTS:

colorful fabric paints

small plates

cotton swabs

stamps made of craft foam, available at craft stores

Wash and press the onesies or T-shirts.

For embroidery, follow the instructions on page 17 to transfer the design from an embroidery template onto the onesie or T-shirt. Chain stitch (see page 15) along pattern lines. See pages 13–17 for more stitch ideas and instructions.

For appliqués, position decoration on the right side of the fabric. Working from the wrong side, bring the needle up through the fabric and make a small stitch through the back side of the appliqué, not bringing the needle all the way to the surface. Repeat, attaching the decoration securely in multiple places, especially near the edges, so it cannot be removed. Use a pin-prick stitch (see page 16) to attach ribbon and trimming.

For paint prints, lay a onesie on a hard, flat surface and insert a piece of paper, wax paper, or plastic inside the garment to prevent paints from seeping through to the back side. Smooth out any wrinkles. Squirt small dollops of paint onto the plates and use cotton swabs to evenly coat the surface of the stamps with paint. With a steady hand, gently place the stamp in the desired position and apply firm and direct pressure from above, trying not to rock or shift the stamp. Gently remove the stamp by lifting it straight up. Once dry, some paints may need to be ironed in order to set. Follow the manufacturer's instructions.

snuggle suit

A soft snuggle suit made from fleece is a warm and convenient alternative to a blanket when traipsing around town. High-quality fleece is reversible and doesn't fray, making this gift easy to put together, with minimal finishing work.

Photocopy the templates onto plain white paper, enlarging 200 percent. Cut out. Spread out the fleece, pin the template pieces to it, and cut out, following template directions. Remove pins.

Baste the body pieces together along the shoulders and sew, leaving a ⅝-inch seam allowance. Match each sleeve to an armhole, with the center of the curved edge lining up with the shoulder seam, and pin (see illustration). Baste, remove pins, and sew, leaving a ⅝ inch seam allowance. Remove all basting thread. Starting at the cuff, baste the sleeves closed along the length of the arm, turning at the underarm and continuing down the sides of the suit. Sew, leaving a ⅝-inch seam allowance, along the basted edge. Remove basting thread. Trim the seam allowances with the pinking shears and press the seams open. Choose one side to be the front of the suit, and use the straight scissors to make a 6-inch cut down the center of the front, perpendicular to the neck line. This is the neck opening.

To make the hood, baste the two pieces together along the curved edge. Sew, leaving a ⅝-inch seam allowance. Remove basting thread. Trim the seam with the pinking shears and press open. Turn the hood right-side out.

With the hood right-side out and the body inside out, fit the hood down inside the neck hole of the body, matching up the raw edges around the neck and centering the back seam of the hood with the center of the neckline on the body. Pin the hood to the suit. Baste, remove pins, and sew, leaving a ⅝-inch seam allowance. Remove basting thread. Trim all the seams with the pinking shears and press open. Turn the suit right-side out and roll up the sleeves.

templates (pages 104–105)

1 yard reversible fleece

pinking shears, zigzag or scalloped edge

scissors

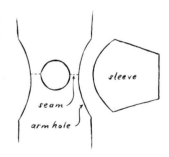

clothes hanger covers

Beautiful baby clothes should be shown off whenever possible. Make fabric- and ribbon-trimmed slipcovers for child-size wooden clothes hangers. These creative covers can be either machine or hand sewn.

wooden baby clothing hangers

½ yard heavy cotton fabric or broadcloth

pinking shears

colorful trims and ribbons

seam ripper or nail scissors

To make a template, place a hanger on a sheet of 8½-by-11-inch paper and trace along the top, marking the exact center. Trace along the sides and continue the line down about 4½ inches, then draw a bottom line. Extend the drawing by ¾ inch on the top and across the sides to allow room for seams. Adjust the length of the template to make hanger covers different lengths to suit a variety of different clothing styles.

Use the template to cut two pieces of fabric for each hanger and baste together, leaving a ⅛-inch seam allowance, up both sides and across the top. Sew, leaving a ⅝-inch seam allowance. Remove the basting thread, trim the seam to ¼ inch, and clip corners, being careful not to cut the stitches (see page 15). Turn the cover to the right side, trim the bottom edge with pinking shears and fold it under ½ inch all the way around. Press the cover.

Using a pin-prick stitch, sew a band of decorative ribbon or trim around the bottom. Use the seam ripper or nail scissors to clip a ½-inch opening at the center of the top seam, then backstitch on either side of the opening to secure stitches. Slip the hanger into the cover, with the hook coming up through the opening on the top.

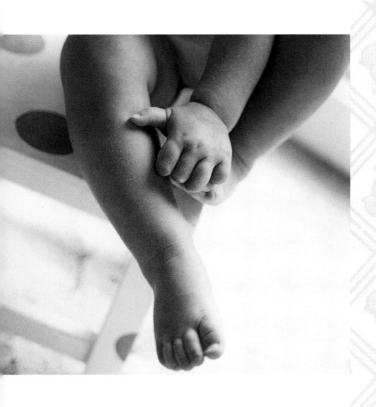

CHAPTER TWO

nursery

TRIMMINGS

silky quilt

A quilt made from silk is a luxurious gift, certainly one we are not likely to buy for ourselves. If silk and baby seems too frivolous a mix, make this quilt from any fabric, such as chenille, soft jersey, or squares cut from vintage tablecloths. Choose polyester or cotton batting—each has its advantages. Polyester is easier to work with, more lightweight, washable, and hypoallergenic. It does not iron well, however, and may fuse to the silk when pressing. Use a very cool iron and test a swatch of silk and batting. If necessary, iron through a pillowcase to protect the fabric and prevent fusing. Cotton batting irons much better but is heavier, not as even in texture, and is best dry-cleaned.

2 yards 45-inch-wide polyester or cotton batting

2 yards 45-inch-wide china silk or raw silk, cut in half, or 1 yard each of two colors

6 skeins silk, cotton, or linen embroidery thread to match

embroidery needle

Cut the batting into two rectangles, each 36 inches by 45 inches, the same size as the fabric pieces. Match and pin a batting rectangle to the wrong side of a silk rectangle and baste with long stitches all the way around. Remove pins. Repeat to baste the remaining batting rectangle to the remaining silk rectangle.

Cut a length of embroidery thread, separate a single strand, thread the needle, and double knot the ends together. Beginning at one corner, 3 inches in from either edge along the shorter side of the quilt, insert the needle up through the batting to the silk side and make a small stitch, slightly larger than a pin-prick stitch (see page 16). Sewing across the

continued

shorter side, make the next stitch two inches from the first and continue at the same spacing, stopping 3 inches from the opposite edge, for a total of 16 stitches. Repeat to make a parallel row of stitches 2 inches from the first row. Continue in this fashion until the entire piece is quilted, for a total of 20 rows of stitches, leaving a 3-inch border all the way around. Remove basting threads. Repeat to quilt the second piece of silk and batting.

Match up the 2 quilted pieces, silk-sides facing. Pin the edges all the way around and then baste, leaving a 2-inch seam allowance. Remove pins. Use a long stitch setting on the sewing machine and, working very slowly, gently begin stitching through all thicknesses, leaving a 1-inch seam allowance. Sew around the four edges of the quilt, leaving an 8-inch opening on one side. Remember to backstitch at beginning and end of the opening.

Turn the quilt right-side out through the opening and make sure all the seams are aligned and no tucks in the fabric have occurred. If you find tucks—small accidental folds that were stitched down—turn the quilt inside out again, clip out the seams where the fabric is tucking, and restitch. Once the seams are perfect, with the quilt inside out, remove all the basting threads. Trim the seams to ¼ inch and clip the corners (see page 15). Turn the quilt right-side out and gently press the seams all the way around—remember to protect silk with a pillowcase if using polyester batting. Close up the 8-inch opening with a slip stitch (see page 17).

painted dresser & polka-dot chair

A baby's nursery can never have too many drawers or surfaces for all the cute little things we accumulate for them. Just a little paint or decoupage and some decorative trimmings will transform your flea-market finds, whether they're grown-up furniture or pint-sized versions. One doesn't need a flair for fine art to add some colorful shapes, designs, or letters to a small dresser, chair, or any other piece of furniture.

Working on the drop cloth to minimize any potential mess, remove all drawers and knobs from the piece of furniture if necessary. Wipe the furniture down to remove any dirt or grime, then lightly sand the surface to ensure that the new coat of paint will stick. Use a 3-inch brush and the pastel semi-gloss to paint the entire surface of the furniture. Allow to dry and apply a second coat if needed. If using decoupage and tissue paper cutouts, paint the furniture white to get the brightest effect from the paper. Allow to dry completely, and apply a second coat if needed.

For the surface of a table or dresser top or for the doors of an armoire, use the masking tape to mark off a 3-inch border all the way around, and paint it white. Allow to dry, and apply second coat if needed. Once the paint is dry, use the stencils and acrylics to paint letters or designs along the border. Put on the whole alphabet, baby's name, or a border of ribbons and bows.

For decoupaging the chair with polka dots, create a template by tracing a jar or drinking-glass bottom onto plain white paper. Cut out the template.

drop cloth

fine-grain sandpaper

3-inch-wide paintbrush

water-based semi-gloss interior paint:
  1 quart pastel
  1 quart white

masking tape

several small watercolor brushes

letter stencils or other stencil designs

acrylic paints in complementary colors

continued

Fold the tissue paper into accordion layers, making sure the width of the accordion is at least 2 inches. Place the polka-dot template on top of the folded tissue and trace. Cut out the polka-dot shape. Continue tracing and cutting until you have enough polka dots to cover your chair (or other item as desired). Alternatively, cut polka dots in varying sizes.

Following the instructions on the container of matte medium, use the ½-inch paintbrush to apply the polka dots all over the chair, making sure to smooth them out flat as you work. Allow to dry completely before using.

When the furniture is thoroughly dry, replace drawers and knobs if necessary.

FOR DECOUPAGE:

jar or glass

colored tissue-paper sheets

decoupage medium, such as Mod-Podge (also called matte medium)

½-inch soft-bristle paintbrush

pom-pom pillow

If you have an inkling of the nursery theme or colors, surprise parents with corresponding pillows for the rocking chair, love seat, or crib. Fun colors and prints make these small pillows an adorable (and very easy) gift. Be sure to keep this pillow out of the crib or anywhere else the baby may be unsupervised.

1⅔ yards matching pom-pom trim

two 15-inch squares of fabric

polyester filling

Baste the seam edge of the pom-pom trim all around the edge of one of the fabric squares on the right side of the fabric, with the pom-poms facing inward, lying on the fabric.

Match up the 2 squares of fabric, right-sides facing, so the pom-pom trim is sandwiched between the squares. Baste edges together, leaving a ½-inch seam allowance, but stop when 5 inches remain. Sew, leaving a ⅜-inch seam allowance, stopping at the opening. Backstitch ½ inch at beginning and end. Remove basting thread.

Clip the corners (see page 15), being careful not to cut the seam. Turn right-side out through the opening and press. Stuff with the polyester filling and slip-stitch the opening closed (see page 17).

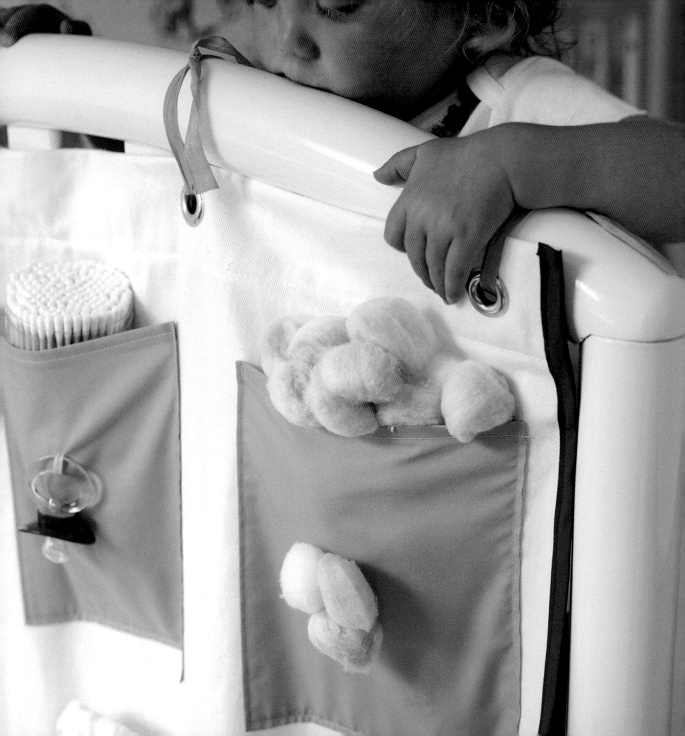

tidy-up nursery organizer

Create a little extra storage by hanging this organizer on a closet door or tying it to the end of a crib. Extra diapers, socks, or anything that needs to be readily accessible will find a niche in one of the pockets. Or, buy a hanging shoe-organizer and decorate pockets with accents to indicate the contents.

Lay the interfacing along one 28-inch side of the canvas. Iron on following the manufacturer's instructions. Allow to cool. Fold the interfaced edge over ½ inch and then again by 2¼ inches. Press and pin. Stitch down, close to the inside edge, and remove pins.

Place 4 eyelets along the finished edge of the canvas, spacing them evenly across, with the 2 end eyelets 1½ inches from the organizer sides. Working on a hard surface, attach the eyelets using the anvil, stud, and hammer according to the eyelet kit instructions.

To make the pockets, fold under all 4 edges of each fabric square by ¼ inch and press. For the smaller pockets, fold one shorter edge over again by ¼ inch and stitch down. For the larger pockets, fold down a 12-inch edge and stitch as above.

Hand sew decorations to the pockets, using either a pin-prick stitch (see page 16) for fabric items or, if stitching will show, three strands of embroidery thread and a simple straight stitch. To attach a small rattle or pacifier, use a series of loop-like stitches around the center of the handle.

Evenly space 3 of the smaller pockets in a row beneath the eyelets, hemmed edges pointing upwards, and pin in place. Repeat this process with the

continued

fusible interfacing, one 4-by-28-inch strip

36-by-28-inch rectangle medium-weight canvas or other strong fabric

kit for making large eyelets (includes metal anvil and stud)

hammer

½ yard light- to medium-weight fabric, 45 inches wide, cut into six 9½-by-8-inch rectangles and two 12-by-8-inch rectangles

decorations such as infant socks and bonnets, diaper pins, pacifiers, felt for cutouts, iron-on appliqués, cute buttons

embroidery thread in assorted colors, optional

3 yards double-fold bias tape, cut into two 37-inch pieces and one 28-inch piece

remaining pockets, creating 2 rows of 3 small pockets and a bottom row of 2 large pockets. Sew the unhemmed edges to the canvas and remove pins.

To complete the organizer, fit the two 37-inch pieces of bias tape along either side, fold the ends under, and pin and sew in place. Repeat with the remaining 28-inch piece along the bottom edge.

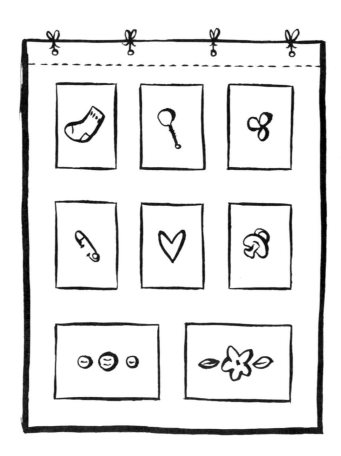

happy hamper

A load of laundry a day, if not two, is just one of many things a new baby brings to a household. Hang a small, colorful hamper from the end of the changing table or crib to collect the daily washing.

Match up a 19-inch edge of the cotton with a 19-inch edge of the canvas, right sides of fabric facing. Pin in place, baste, remove pins, and sew, leaving a ⅜ inch seam allowance. Remove basting thread. Open and iron the seam flat.

You now have one long piece, part canvas and part cotton. Fold the long piece in half lengthwise, wrong-side out, then pin and baste the long edge to secure. Remove pins. Sew the long raw edge closed, leaving a ⅜-inch seam allowance, to form a fabric tube. Remove basting thread. Trim the seam to ¼ inch and press open.

Begin turning the tube inside out, folding the canvas part of the hamper down over the cotton fabric, until the raw edges meet. The right side of the canvas fabric will be facing outward, with the cotton inside. Flatten the tube into a rectangle, with the seam running down the center of one face. Pin along the raw edge at bottom and sew straight through all thicknesses, leaving a ⅜-inch seam allowance. Remove pins, trim seam allowance to ¼ inch, and press seam open.

To square off the bottom of the hamper, stand the hamper up and pinch the bottom corners to form triangles perpendicular to the sides (see illustration, page 52). Measure 3 inches in from one corner point along the bottom seam and sew across the corner. Cut off excess material, leaving a ¼-inch seam allowance, and clip the corner (see page 15). Repeat process with the opposite corner. Turn the hamper cotton-side out.

36-by-19-inch rectangle of medium-weight cotton fabric

25-by-19-inch rectangle of medium- to heavy-weight canvas for lining

2 yards 2½-inch-wide silk, satin, or other type of ribbon, cut into two pieces, one 45 inches long and one 27 inches long

continued

To create a tunnel for the ribbon drawstring, sew a seam around the circumference of the hamper opening, just below the seam where the cotton meets the canvas. Sew another seam 1½ inches below the first. Use a seam ripper to open the small section of the vertical seam that lies between the two drawstring seams you just made.

Attach a large safety pin to one end of the 45-inch length of the ribbon and thread it through the seam opening. Work the safety pin through the tunnel, drawing the ribbon along with it. Pull to cinch. This is the front of the hamper.

To make the hanging ties, fold the remaining length of ribbon in half. Center the ribbon vertically along the back center seam, positioning the fold point over the drawstring seams, and sew in place above and below the drawstring seams.

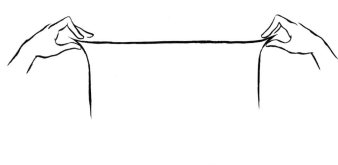

cut off excess

sew pinched ends

everything baskets

These versatile baskets can be used for nearly anything, from toiletries to cotton balls, clean sheets to stray toys—you name it. Durable oilcloth linings wipe clean and stand up to the wear and tear of daily use. Armed with a measuring tape, you can make custom liners for just about any basket, although flat-bottomed ones with straight sides are the easiest to work with. Make a bevy of baskets for strategic placement around the house.

To make a pattern for the basket lining, start by measuring the bottom of the basket, then add 1¼ inch to all sides and cut a piece of paper to fit. For the sides of the basket, measure the interior depth and add 2½ inches, then measure the exterior perimeter of the basket top and add 1 inch; cut a rectangle of paper to these dimensions.

Pin each pattern piece to the fabric and cut out, leaving a ⅜-inch margin of fabric all around each template. Remove pins.

To finish the top edge of the liner, turn over an edge of the side lining piece ½ inch and sew it down, stitching very close to the inner edge.

To attach the bottom to the side piece, lay the bottom piece of fabric out flat, right side of fabric facing upward. Pin the long piece along the edges of the bottom piece, right sides of fabric facing. Where the ends of the side lining meet at one of the bottom corners, leave enough fabric overlapping to sew a ⅜-inch seam up the lining side. Sew all along the pinned edge, removing the pins as you go, being careful not to sew over them. Sew up the side, leaving a ⅜-inch seam. Trim the seams to ¼ inch. Center a decorative button along the edge of each liner side and sew in place on the right side of the fabric. Slide the liner inside the basket and fold the edge snugly over the basket top.

several tight-weave square baskets without handles

1 to 2 yards oilcloth in various colors or patterns

4 vintage or oversized buttons for each basket

nighty night-light

A socket night-light fitted with a tiny half-shade provides just a hint of light to a cozy nursery. Inexpensive night-lights are available in most hardware stores and drugstores and are usually fitted with a 4-watt bulb. Replace the existing bulb with a small 15-watt bulb. This low-wattage bulb will not damage delicate paper- or fabric-covered shades, so your possibilities are limitless.

1 ready-made half lamp-shade frame (4 to 6 inches), to fit a small bulb

fabric, paper, or wallpaper

½-inch-wide adhesive linen tape (found in craft stores)

15-watt flame-tip bulb

1 small socket night-light with plastic bulb-cover removed

Measure the height and the top and bottom perimeters of the lamp-shade frame, as it may taper slightly from the top to the bottom. Add ⅛ inch to each perimeter measurement and draw a shape corresponding to the 3 dimensions on a piece of plain white paper. Using the paper template, cut out a piece of paper or fabric to cover the shade frame.

Cut lengths of linen tape to fit along all the edges of the shade frame. Lay the fabric or paper out flat, right-side up, and carefully place a matching strip of tape along the edge that will be the top, leaving ¼ inch of the tape width free. Fit the taped edge along the top of the frame and fold the remaining ¼ inch of tape over to the back side of the frame, pressing firmly as you go. Do the same for the bottom edge and sides, pulling taut as you work. Where necessary, pinch the ends of the tape together and trim. Screw the 15-watt bulb into the socket night-light, clip the shade to the bulb, and plug in the night-light.

CHAPTER THREE

pretty

PRACTICALITIES

hooded towel

Hooded towels are useful for newborns, who need a little extra swaddling. This project is a cinch to complete using soft terry-cloth bath sheets—extra large bath towels measuring two yards long—and matching washcloths. One bath sheet and one washcloth will make two cuddly hooded towels. Accent with complementary colors of bias tape.

1 package ½-inch double-fold bias tape

1 terry-cloth bath sheet towel cut in half crosswise to make two squarish rectangles

1 terry-cloth washcloth cut in half along the diagonal, making two triangles

Cut a length of bias tape to fit along the diagonal edge of the washcloth triangle. Fit the tape snugly along the edge and baste in place. Sew the bias tape to the terry cloth, as close to the edge of the bias tape as possible, working slowly to maintain a nice, straight stitching line. Remove basting thread.

Pin the point of the triangle to a corner of the bath-sheet half, matching up the right angles, and baste in place. Remove pins. Cut a length of bias tape to fit around the perimeter of the towel. Fit the tape snugly around the towel edges, including where the hood is attached, and baste in place. Machine stitch the bias tape to the towel, sewing close to the edge of the tape. Fold the overlapping end of the bias tape under and sew down, backstitching ¼ inch to secure. Trim any loose threads.

bring-along bassinet

A friend of mine kept her newborn in a handheld baby basket for his first couple of months, switching to a crib only later, as her son began to squirm around more actively. Find an inexpensive or used bassinet in an antique or secondhand store and replace the bedding with luxurious cotton piqué or damask. If your bassinet doesn't come with a pad or is used, cut one to fit from a plastic changing pad.

Using the bassinet mattress pad as a template, cut 2 pieces of white cotton piqué or damask in the shape of the pad, but add 3 inches to the width and 4 inches to the length. Set one piece aside.

Cut the remaining fabric piece in half crosswise, creating 2 half-oval pieces of fabric. Fold over the newly cut edges of each half ¼ inch and press. Fold over again ½ inch and press. Sew the pressed edges down, stitching ⅛ inch from the edge.

Place the 2 pieces on the remaining large oval piece with their hemmed edges meeting in the middle, and trim the larger piece to fit the 2 smaller ones. Pin the pieces together, right sides of fabric facing, and baste with a ½-inch seam allowance all around the outer edge, creating a slipcover for the pad. Remove pins, sew, and trim the seams to ⅜ inch. Remove basting thread, press the slipcover, and fit it over the pad.

For the bottom lining, use the mattress pad as a template again, add ½ inch all the way around, and cut an oval of fabric to fit. Set aside.

wicker or straw oval bassinet, original fabric and linens removed

3 yards white cotton piqué or damask

2 packages white, ¼-inch-wide double-fold bias tape

1½ yards ¼-inch-wide silk ribbon cut into six 9-inch pieces

1 yard 4-inch-wide white ribbon, grosgrain or satin

hot-glue gun and glue

continued

For the side lining, measure the circumference of the top edge of the basket and add 10 inches. Measure the depth of the bassinet and add 5 inches, so the lining will hang over the edges of the bassinet when finished. Cut two rectangles of fabric to these dimensions. Match the two pieces up, right sides of fabric facing. Baste the short edges together at each end and sew, leaving a ⅜-inch seam allowance. Remove basting thread.

Set the sewing machine to the longest straight stitch and, leaving the lining inside out, sew a running stitch (see page 16) across one long side of the rectangle, about ½ inch from the edge. Pull on one of the stitch threads at the end of the seam to gather the fabric. Gather the fabric until the rectangle is small enough to fit around the edge of the basket-bottom piece. Turn right-side out.

With the right sides of the fabric facing, pin the gathered edge of the rectangle around the edge of the bottom piece of fabric. Baste, leaving a ½-inch seam allowance, and remove pins. Sew along the basted edges with a ⅜-inch seam allowance. Remove basting thread.

Fit the lining inside the bassinet, wrong side of fabric facing the inside of the basket. Fit the mattress pad inside, on top of the lining. Sizes and shapes of bassinet vary, so you may need to trim extra fabric from the lining edge. Let the excess hang over 3½ inches all the way around.

Remove the lining and finish the edge by fitting the bias tape snugly along the unsewn edge and stitching it to the lining. Overlap the end of the bias tape, tuck it under, and sew the folded end down to finish. Press the lining and fit it inside the bassinet.

Fold each of the six 9-inch lengths of ribbon in half and use a pin-prick stitch (see page 16) to hand sew the fold points to the top edge of the lining, one piece at each end of the bassinet and one piece next to each end of both handles. Slip one end of each ribbon piece in and around the weave of the wicker or straw 3 inches down the outside, and tie the lining in place. Let the fabric bunch softly around the handles. Snugly fit the pad down inside the bassinet.

Wrap the handles with the 4-inch-wide ribbon, gluing the ribbon ends in place to secure.

beach-ready diaper tote

For a quick beach tote, wrap the shoulder straps of an ordinary straw bag with soft velvet ribbon, then make a small travel-size changing pad from colorful Mexican oilcloth. Fill the bag with necessities, and Mom and Dad will be ready to go.

Use the hot-glue gun to attach one end of a 60-inch length of ribbon to the end of one of the straps on the bag. Wrap the ribbon around the strap in a spiral fashion, covering it completely, and glue it at the other end. Trim off any excess. Repeat process for the other strap. Tie the remaining 4 pieces of ribbon over each glued end of the straps and trim the ends at an angle.

To make the changing pad, sandwich the foam piece between the two pieces of oilcloth, right sides of fabric facing outward, and pin all three pieces together. Fold the ½-inch-wide cord or ribbon in half and slip about 1 inch of the folded end into the sandwich at the center point of a shorter side. Pin to secure, then sew all the way around the perimeter of the pad, leaving a ¼-inch seam allowance. Trim the edges with the pinking shears, being careful not to clip the cord.

Fold the pad into thirds and tie with the attached cord. Slip the pad into the bag with the rest of the goodies.

Fill the bag with a few diapers, a pacifier, a self-sealing sandwich bag filled with wipes, 45-spf UVA/UVB sunblock, and a small baby towel. For fun, add in a few small beach toys, such as a shovel and bucket. Don't forget a beach novel or other light reading for grown-ups.

FOR THE BAG:

hot-glue gun and glue

4 yards 2-inch-wide velvet ribbon, preferably in a shade of lime or mango, cut into two 60-inch pieces and four 6-inch pieces

large straw bag with shoulder straps

FOR THE TRAVEL CHANGING PAD:

25-by-14-inch rectangle of ½-inch-thick headliner foam (available in craft or fabric store upholstery departments)

1 yard of oilcloth, cut into two 25-by-14-inch rectangles

1 yard of ½-inch-wide cord or ribbon

pinking shears

embroidered nursing cloths

An abundance of nursing cloths is just what a new mom needs to wipe up little burps and spills. Mismatched vintage white damask napkins, found in thrift stores, flea markets, and antique shops, make perfect nursing cloths, an elegant alternative to using cloth diapers for this purpose. Find embroidery templates in your local craft or fabric store, and use them as guides to embroider simple designs onto one corner of each napkin.

3 embroidery templates (page 103)

3 or more vintage damask napkins (Irish linens are especially nice)

cotton embroidery thread

embroidery needle

Follow the instructions on page 17 to transfer the design from an embroidery template onto one corner of one napkin, keeping it within a 4-inch square. Repeat to transfer remaining designs onto remaining napkins.

Fill in the design, using the chain stitch for letters and outlines, the satin stitch for filling in shapes, and French knots for a nubby texture (see pages 15–16 for stitch instructions).

Press the napkins, avoiding the embroidery, so as not to flatten the new work. Fold the cloths into squares with the embroidery patterns on top.

flannel receiving blanket

A receiving blanket is for baby's days in the hospital and the first couple of weeks at home. This soft, cuddly version is simply made with two squares of flannel sewn together. Make several in different colors and prints and bundle together with ribbon.

Cut the flannel into two 1-yard squares and match up the squares, right-sides facing. Pin the squares together and then baste all around the edges, leaving a 5-inch-long opening. Remove pins. Sew, leaving a ⅜-inch seam allowance, along the basted edges, stopping at the opening. Backstitch ½ inch at beginning and end. Remove basting thread. Trim the seams to ¼ inch and clip all 4 corners (see page 15).

Turn the blanket right-side out through the opening and use the tip of a pin to gently pull the corners into points. Press the edges of the blanket and slip-stitch the opening closed (see page 17).

2 yards double-sided flannel, different colors if desired

changing pad and sheets

Customize an ordinary plastic changing pad by sewing fitted flannel sheets for it. It only takes 1½ yards of fabric to make two sheets, so it's easy to whip up enough of them to get new parents through a few days with no laundry.

1½ yards flannel, 45 inches or wider

seam ripper

two 13-inch pieces of ¼-inch-wide elastic

1-inch-thick rectangular changing pad, about 34 by 15 inches

Use scissors to round off the four corners of the flannel piece. Fold all edges under ½ inch and press. Fold edges under again ¼ inch, pressing as you go. Pin edges and sew the hem down by machine, stitching very close to the inner edge. Remove pins.

Fold the sheet in half lengthwise, right-side in. On one end of the sheet, place the end of a measuring tape flush with the fold and measure 11 inches along the sewn edge. Mark this point with a pencil. Repeat at the other end of the sheet. Turn the folded sheet over, and repeat these markings on the opposite side. Unfold. At each marking, use the seam ripper to open up the seam ¼ inch. Backstitch on either side of the opening to secure stitching.

Attach a safety pin to the end of one piece of the elastic and thread it into a seam opening at the top of the sheet. Stitch down the other end of the elastic close to the same seam opening. Thread the elastic through the seam tunnel, away from the center of the sheet and around the two corners to the opposite seam opening. Secure the end of the elastic by stitching it in place where it emerges from the seam opening. Repeat with the second piece of elastic at the opposite end of the sheet.

Slip the elastic corners of the sheet over the corners of the changing pad.

no-sew bibs

Feeding a baby and later teaching one to eat are very messy jobs. These quick and easy wipe-clean bibs are the ideal gift for babies with big appetites. Make a whole stack of them in different colors and patterns.

Photocopy the template onto plain white paper, enlarging 200 percent. Cut out and set aside.

Following the manufacturer's directions, apply the iron-on vinyl square to the right side of the fabric square. Set aside the protective paper.

When the vinyl has cooled, pin the template to the fabric and cut out. Remove pins.

Cut lengths of fusible tape to match the lengths of bias tape. Use your fingertips to gently press the fusible tape to the wrong side of each piece of bias tape.

Fit the shorter length of bias tape over the neckline edge of the bib, pressing gently to make it adhere to both sides. Cover the bib with the protective paper, then iron it, following the ironing instructions for the fusible tape.

Fit the longer piece of bias tape around the bib, leaving equal lengths extending on both sides of the neck to create the ties. Press gently to make the tape adhere to the edge of the bib, and iron as above.

For an even sturdier, longer-lasting bib, use a ¼-inch-wide double-fold bias tape and machine stitch it down.

template (page 100)

11-inch square of clear iron-on vinyl, matte or gloss

12-inch square of lightweight cotton in a fun and colorful print (⅓ yard of 60-inch-wide fabric makes 5 bibs)

½-inch-wide double-stick fusible tape, such as Steam-a-Seam

1 yard matching ½-inch-wide single-fold bias tape, cut into one 7¼-inch piece and one 28¾-inch piece

28 7/16"

baby bath kit

A gift made up of practical elements artfully presented is fun to create and always appreciated. For a baby's bath kit, select useful items such as a first toothbrush, a thermometer, washcloths, and a rubber ducky.

1 soft terry-cloth towel

baby thermometer

teething rattle, rubber duck, or other toys

baby toothbrush

pacifier

washcloth

more baby toiletries such as hairbrush, sunscreen, bubble bath, bath milk, baby shampoo, skin creams

1 yard 4-inch-wide ribbon

Fold the towel into thirds lengthwise and begin rolling it into a tube. Place one of the items partially in the towel, roll a bit, and place another item. Continue until all the little gifts are snugly tucked into the towel, but sticking out slightly. Wrap the ribbon around the towel and tie in a bow.

CHAPTER FOUR

toys

AND THINGS

ABCs

Puffy alphabet letters spelling out the ABCs or a baby's name are a delightful addition to any nursery wall, crib end, cupboard, or closet door. A little spot of self-adhesive Velcro enables them to stick to a number of surfaces. Create your own letter templates in any style and size, or find letter stencils in an art store to use as guides.

On a piece of white paper, draw a rectangle approximately 9 inches high and 5 inches wide. In this rectangle, sketch your chosen letter at the desired thickness, sizing the letter to abut the edges of the rectangle. Using the red pen, outline your letter, leaving a ⅜-inch margin all the way around. Cut out the letter along the red lines. Pin the letter template to the felt, cut out, and remove pins. Repeat, flipping the template to create a mirror image. Match up the fabric letter cutouts and pin to secure.

Cut a 1-yard length of embroidery thread and separate three strands. Thread the needle and knot the thread at one end. Sew the letter pieces together with a ¼-inch straight stitch, leaving a ⅜-inch seam allowance and a 2-inch opening. Remove pins, trim the edges with the pinking shears, stuff the letter with the polyester filling, and stitch the opening closed.

Stick one side of the Velcro to the back of the letter; hot-glue in place if needed. Stick the opposite piece of Velcro to the surface where you want the letter to hang.

Repeat to make more letters as desired.

red pen

felt in bright colors

cotton embroidery thread

embroidery needle

pinking shears (optional)

polyester filling

1-inch squares of self-adhesive Velcro

hot-glue gun and glue

squeezable blocks

These squishy blocks are ideal for a baby who is just getting a handle on reaching and grabbing. Mix and match fabrics and make blocks in all different sizes, so baby can practice a little preliminary stacking and building.

TO MAKE 3 BLOCKS:

3 pieces cotton fabric in different colors, ¼ yard each

polyester filling

To make block templates, draw a 5½-inch square, a 4½-inch square, and a 3½-inch square on plain white paper. Cut out the templates.

For each soft block, cut 6 same-size squares of fabric, using the templates as your guide. Press any wrinkles or creases out of the fabric.

Baste 4 of the 6 squares in a row, side by side, leaving a ½-inch seam allowance. Baste the 2 remaining squares to each side of the second square in the longer row, creating a lowercase "t" shape (see illustration, page 84).

Sew, leaving a ¼-inch seam allowance, along all basted edges. Remove basting thread. Press seams flat.

With the "t" shape lying flat, right side of fabric up, bring the first square in the long row and one of the side squares in the short row perpendicular to the rest of the fabric. Pin along the meeting edges. Bring the remaining side square in the short row perpendicular and pin, creating the bottom and three sides of a cube. Baste, leaving a ½-inch seam allowance, and remove pins.

continued

Sew, leaving a ¼-inch seam allowance, along all basted edges. Remove basting thread. Close up the cube, pinning and basting the remaining two squares to the sides and top. Remove pins and sew as before, but leaving a 2-inch opening somewhere along the final seam. Be sure all pins and basting thread have been removed.

Turn the cube right-side out. Press along the seams to form a tidy cube shape. Fill with the polyester filling, overstuffing for a firm shape and understuffing for a softer block. Slip-stitch the opening closed (see page 17).

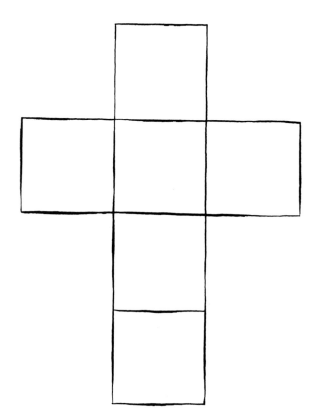

snuggle bear blanket

This all-in-one stuffed bear and blanket will quickly become a favorite toy. Soft reversible fleece is washable, meaning easy care for Mom and Dad, and has no wrong or right side, meaning easy work for the crafter.

Photocopy the template pieces onto plain white paper, enlarging 200 percent. Cut out.

Cut two 26-inch-by-18-inch pieces of fabric, long sides running with the grain of the fabric. Set aside.

Pin the templates for the head, torso, and ears to the remaining piece of fabric and cut out. Remove pins. Cut out the eyes, nose, and mouth lines from the face template, using a utility knife with a fresh blade if necessary. Use the disappearing-ink marker to trace the cutout areas onto the face fabric. Remove the template.

To embroider the face, cut a 1-yard length of embroidery thread and separate three strands. Use the satin stitch (see page 16) to fill in the eyes and nose, then use a chain stitch (see page 15) to outline the mouth, using more thread as needed.

To make the ears, match up 2 ear pieces and baste together along the curved edge, leaving the bottom unsewn. Sew, leaving a ¼-inch seam allowance, along the basted edges, and clip the seams several times around the curves (see page 15). Remove basting thread. Repeat to create second ear; turn the ears right-side out so the seams are on the inside.

templates (pages 106–107)

1 yard 60-inch-wide reversible fleece

disappearing-ink marker

embroidery thread

polyester stuffing

continued

Working with the embroidered head piece, position the ears on either side of the head top, each about 1½ inches from the center, the raw bottom edges lying along the top edge of the head. The ears will be lying on the face of the bear. Place the remaining head piece atop the ears, right side facing the embroidered face, sandwiching the ears between the head pieces. Pin the pieces in place and baste the head together around the circumference, leaving a 3-inch opening at the bottom for the neck hole. Remove pins, sew with a ⅜-inch seam allowance along the basted edge, and clip the seam every 1½ inches (see page 15). Remove basting thread and turn the head right-side out.

To make the body, pin the two torso pieces together, right-sides in. Baste the sides together, leaving the bottom open and a 3-inch opening for the neck. Remove pins. Sew with a ⅜-inch seam allowance along the basted edges and clip the finished seam around the curves of the arms. Remove basting thread. Leave the torso inside out.

To attach the head to the torso, slip the head inside the body, matching up the neck hole openings. Baste the pieces together and sew, leaving a ⅜-inch seam allowance. Remove basting thread. Turn the bear right-side out and stuff with the polyester filling until firm. Sew the bottom edge of the body closed.

For the blanket part of the snuggle, match up the two large pieces of fabric, round off the 2 bottom corners with scissors, then pin and baste the sides and bottom. Remove pins. Sew, leaving a ⅜-inch seam allowance, and remove basting thread. Sew a running stitch all around the opening at the top edge of the body, ½ inch from the edge. Pull on one of the stitch threads at the end of the seam to gather the fabric until it fits perfectly around the bottom of the bear body. Fold down the gathered edge of the blanket and slip-stitch it to the body (see page 17).

sleepytime mobile

When sleep seems to elude a baby, a mobile of fuzzy sheep might help lull those little eyes shut. A good fake wool is excellent for this project; if you can find it, unspun lamb's wool or wool pile adds a touch of authenticity.

Photocopy the sheep and fence templates onto plain white paper, enlarging 100 percent. Cut out. Place the templates on the foam and trace around them with a pen. You'll be able to see the outline on the black foam. Repeat to trace a total of 6 sheep and 6 fences. Cut out the shapes.

Tie the end of a piece of filament to the top center of one fence. Then wrap the filament around the midsection of one sheep, about 2 inches above the fence. Pair up the remaining 5 sheep and fences, and repeat filament procedure for each.

Cut squares of the wool large enough to cover the sheep bodies; only the head, tail, and legs should show. Thread the filament through the needle and pull it through the center of a square of wool. Slip the wool down the filament and glue it over both sides of the sheep body.

Tie each strand of filament to the embroidery ring at varying lengths, and hang from the ceiling out of baby's reach.

templates (page 108)

black craft foam

pen

one reel of clear filament; cut six 20-inch strands

fake wool

large-eye needle

hot-glue gun and glue

12-inch embroidery ring, interior piece only

soft-page baby book

Colorful felt is the basis for this very simple book babies seem to love. A decorative blanket stitch binds it together, and vivid cutouts fill the pages.

10 precut felt pieces
(9 by 12 inches)
in a rainbow of colors

large-eye embroidery needle

embroidery thread

Cut four 4-by-12-inch rectangles of felt, each in a different color.

Cut simple shapes from remaining felt as images for the fronts and backs of the pages. Any simple and graphic shape will do: butterfly, train, heart, bug, flower, and alphabet letters. Cut 8 shapes in all.

Thread the embroidery needle with a double strand of thread and knot the ends together. Fold one felt rectangle in half, forming two 6-inch squares joined at the fold. With the fold running on the left side, secure one shape firmly to the center front of the top square with a simple straight stitch around the perimeter of the shape, about ¼ inch from the edge. Do not to stitch through to the bottom square. Flip the page over and with fold running on the right side sew a second felt shape onto the back of the bottom square, again being careful not to stitch through to the front. The back of your stitches will be hidden in between the two squares. Match edges carefully and stitch the two squares together with a simple straight stitch around the three unfolded edges. Repeat to make the remaining 3 pages.

Stack the felt squares, matching the edges carefully. Using the embroidery needle and thread, sew the pages together along the folded edges with a blanket stitch (see page 14).

stamped building blocks

Homemade versions of the classic wooden letter block take very little time or money to create. Hardware stores carry pine square dowels, which the store will cut into cubes on request. Use rubber stamps to decorate all six sides. Take great care to observe all safety instructions when using the polyurethane sealant.

Use the coarse sandpaper to smooth the cut sides of the blocks and gently round the corners and edges. Use the fine sand paper to finish and further smooth the entire block. The blocks must be perfectly slick to the touch. No splinters!

Wearing rubber gloves and using the cotton rag, lightly coat all sides of the blocks except for one with the polyurethane. Set the blocks on the uncoated side and allow to dry until they are just tacky to the touch and can easily be handled (about 1 hour).

When ready, wear rubber gloves and use the cotton rag to coat the remaining side of the blocks. Set the blocks wet-side up and allow to dry (at least 24 hours).

Once the polyurethane is completely dry, stamp the decorations on all sides of the blocks and let the ink dry (at least 24 hours).

coarse and fine grades of sandpaper

10 or more 1½-inch square blocks cut from a wooden dowel

rubber gloves

cotton rag

low-luster polyurethane sealant

rubber stamps

ink pads in various colors

vintage suitcase toy chest

Vintage suitcases make practical storage units for toys. Look for suitcases in antique shops and secondhand stores. Give them a good washing and new lining, and add a pair of sturdy table legs.

small vintage suitcase in good shape

1 quart flat or semi-gloss paint, optional

2-inch paint brush, optional

cotton fabric

4 short table legs with screws attached, available at hardware and lumber stores

wood stain for the legs, optional

electric drill fitted with appropriate drill bit

four bolts to secure legs

spray glue

linen tape

Clean the suitcase with a damp sponge and wipe dry. If necessary, paint the entire surface of the suitcase, let dry and give it a second coat. Measure the interior, then cut pieces of fabric to fit the sides, bottom, and top adding ½ inch to all sides. Fold all the edges of the fabric under by ½ inch and press and set aside.

Before attaching the legs, follow the instructions of the wood stain to color the natural wood, or paint them to match the suitcase. To attach the table legs, drill a hole in each corner of the suitcase bottom. Fit the leg screw through the hole and adjust it so it extends through by ½ inch. To adjust the screw length, begin to unscrew the screw from the leg; this will extend the length. Once the screws are fitted through the bottom of the suitcase, secure them in place with the bolts.

Spray the entire interior of the suitcase with the spray glue and line with the prepared pieces of fabric, matching them up in all the seams and corners. Cover the seams where the fabric pieces match up and along the edges with lengths of the linen tape to give the interior a finished look. The fabric will not lay flat over the bolts on the bottom, but this is easily covered when the toy chest is full of toys.

glossary

BIAS TAPE—Premade cloth finishing tape cut across the grain of fabric so it will smoothly fit along rounded edges. Use to finish seams and raw edges.

GRAIN—The grain is the vertical weave pattern in fabrics, paralleling the selvage.

PINKING SHEARS—Scissors with a zigzag or scalloped edge, used to trim seams and edges in order to prevent fraying.

RIGHT SIDE OF FABRIC—The side of the fabric we see in final products.

SEAM—A line of stitching that holds pieces of fabric together, and the narrow edges of fabric, usually between ¼ and ½ inch wide. Sewing machines have guides to help you sew the appropriate seam width.

SEAM ALLOWANCE—The narrow edge outside the stitching or basting of a seam, usually ⅝ inch wide, which is large enough to trim.

WRONG SIDE OF FABRIC—The back side of a piece of fabric.

CRAFT, ART, AND SEWING SUPPLIES

B and J Fabrics
263 West 40th Street
New York, NY 10018
212-354-8150
fabrics

Bell'occhio
8 Brady Street
San Francisco, CA 94103
415-864-4048
new and vintage ribbons

Britex Fabrics
146 Geary Street
San Francisco, CA 94108
415-392-2910
fabrics, trims, ribbons

**Carter & Company /
Mt. Diablo Handprints**
451 Ryder Street
Vallejo, CA 94590
707-554-2682
www.carterandco.com
historic wallpaper reproductions

Discount Fabrics
San Francisco, CA
415-621-5584
four locations

F and S Fabrics
10629 Wilshire Boulevard
Los Angeles, CA 90064
310-470-3398
fabrics, trims, ribbons

Flax Art and Design
1699 Market Street
San Francisco, CA 94103
415-552-2355
www.flaxart.com
art and craft supplies

**Jo-Ann Fabric and
Crafts**
1-888-739-4120
www.joann.com
fabrics and craft supplies

Lincoln Fabrics
1600 Lincoln Boulevard
Venice, CA 90291
310-396-5724
fabrics, ribbons, trimmings,
some vintage

**Mendel's Far Out
Fabric and Art Supplies**
1556 Haight Street
San Francisco, CA 94117
415-621-1287
fabrics, notions, art, and craft
supplies

**Michael's Arts and
Crafts**
972-409-7660
www.michaels.com
craft supplies

Moskatel's
733 S. San Julian Street
Los Angeles, CA 90014
213-689-4830
craft supplies

Pearl Art Supply
800-451-7327
www.pearlpaint.com
art and craft supplies

Poppy Fabrics
5151 Broadway
Oakland, CA 94611
510-655-5151
fabric, trimmings, some craft
supplies

The Ribbonerie Inc.
191 Potrero Avenue
San Francisco, CA 94103
415-647-0268
ribbons, trims, some vintage

Satin Moon Fabrics
32 Clement Street
San Francisco, CA 94118
415-668-1623
fabrics, trimmings, ribbons

www.shades-n-more.com
lamp shade frames of all sizes
and shapes

Tinsel Trading
47 West 38th Street
New York, NY 10018
212-730-1030
new and vintage trimmings

BABY ACCESSORIES, SUPPLIES, AND CLOTHES

www.ahappyplanet.com
888-946-4277
all-natural, cotton baby clothes
and accessories

Bauerware, Cabinet
and Hardware
3886 17th Street
San Francisco, CA 94110
415-864-3886
www.bauerware.com
cabinet knobs, doorknobs, pulls,
vintage, designer, and one-of-a-
kind items

Forgotten Shanghai
1301 17th Street,
San Francisco, CA 94107
415-701-7707
www.forgottenshanghai.com
furniture, pillows, and room
designs

Grand Remnants
Vintage Textiles
651-222-0221
www.grandremnants.com
vintage textiles and furnishings

Ikea
800-434-4532
www.ikea.com
baby furniture

Maison d'Etre
5640 College Avenue
Oakland, CA 94610
www.maisondetre.com
French antiques, home
furnishings

Marshalls
800-627-7425
www.marshallsonline.com
baby clothes

Pottery Barn
800-588-6250
www.potterybarn.com
home accessories, baby furniture

Target
800-800-8800
www.target.com
baby clothes and
accessories

Tea
358 Addison Avenue
Palo Alto, CA 94301
415-828-9584
baby bedding, clothes,
and room design

FLEA MARKETS

Check your local Chamber
of Commerce for flea
market locations, times,
and dates

Alameda Point Flea
Market
Alameda, CA
510-869-5428

Rose Bowl Flea Market
Pasadena, CA
323-560-7469

Santa Monica Outdoor
Antique Market
Market Place Productions
323-933-2511

acknowledgments

Thank you to my mother, Georgeanne, who taught me how to sew and worked with me on the gifts for this book. Thank you Aura, who helped me make the projects for photography, tested my directions, and learned to embroider. I'd especially like to thank Laurie Frankel, whose love of babies and beautiful things shows in her photographs and design work. Thank you Laurent, my cute husband, who let me craft us out of house and home.

Laurie and I would like to extend our thanks and gratitude to the families who shared their beautiful children with us and to all the people who helped us with photography and lent us their wonderful homes and belongings. Thank you to all the gorgeous babies who patiently let us photograph them, Virgil Warren, Jesse James Philipopoulos, Sascha and Amelia Douglass, Flannery Strain, Ashley Pullen, Mia Alice Rogers, Chloe Durham, Mary Roediger, Zoe Neuschatz, Ethan Ostrow, and Benjamin Michael Abrams.

I would also like to thank Laurie's family, whose sons, Julius and Xander, were our stand-in models, and whose husband, Gary, stood by supportively while we took over the house.

Thank you Bauerware for loaning us furniture hardware; Bell'occhio for constant inspiration and beautiful ribbons; Lily, Daisy, Fred, and Patty of Maison d'Etre for their beautiful French props; Carter and Company/Mt. Diablo Handprints for their vintage reprint wallpapers; Forgotten Shanghai for inspiring and exotic baby-room furniture; and to Shelly and Emily of Tea for all their help and fabulous designs.

Thank you Mikyla Bruder, my amazing and diligent editor; Jodi Davis, for keeping me on track; Elizabeth Bell, for her attention to detail and craft edits; and to our designers, Ben Shaykin and Laura Lovett, who encouraged us along the way.

no-sew bib template

(see page 75)

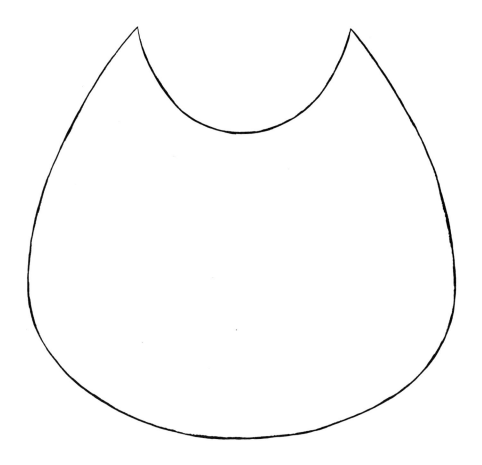

felt cap and booties templates

(see page 27)

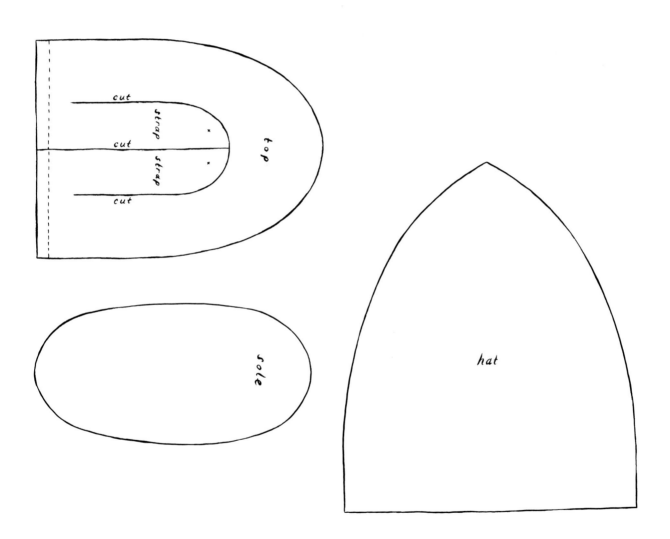

baby bloomers template

(see page 20)

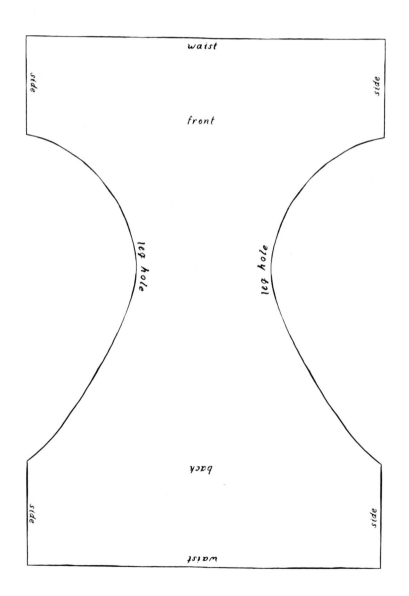

embroidered nursing cloths templates

(see page 68)

snuggle suit templates

(see page 35)

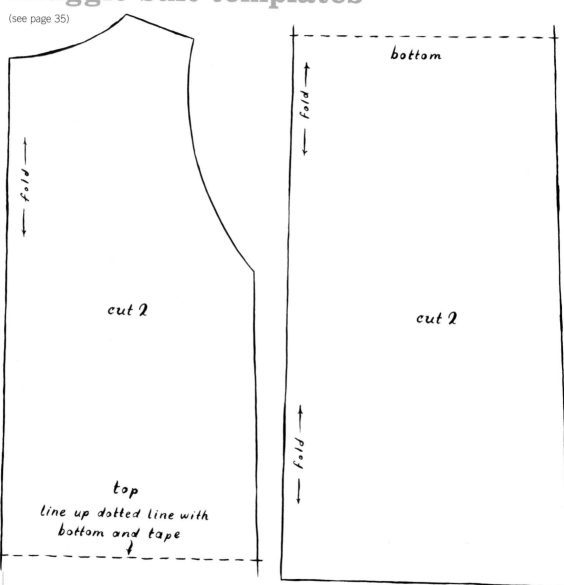

fold

cut 2

top
line up dotted line with
bottom and tape

bottom

fold

cut 2

fold

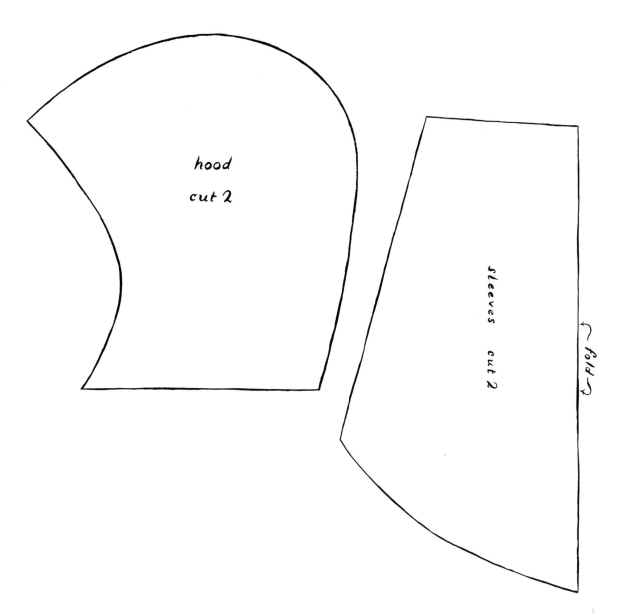

hood

cut 2

sleeves   cut 2

← fold →

snuggle bear blanket templates

(see page 85)

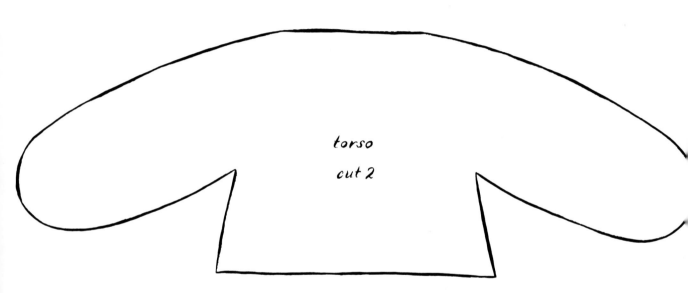

torso

cut 2

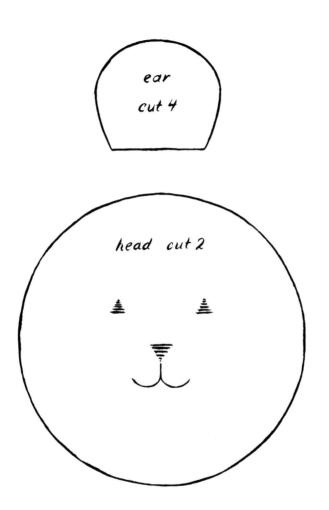

ear

cut 4

head cut 2

sleepytime mobile templates

(see page 89)

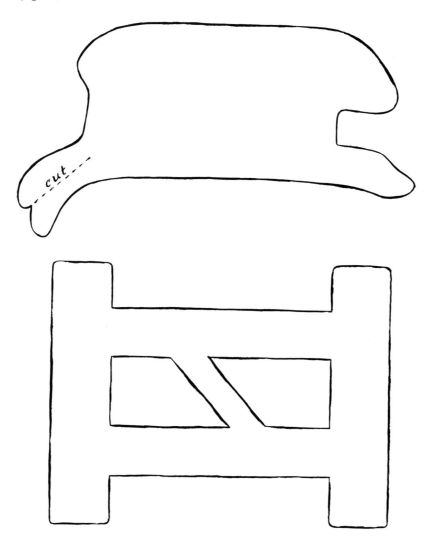

cut

3892